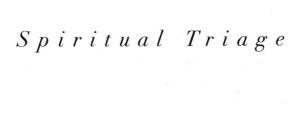

Spiritual Triage

SPIRITUAL TRIAGE

Timely Meditations
for Health-care Workers

Kaaren **Nowicki**

RESOURCE *Publications* · Eugene, Oregon

FOR

Cheryl, who said, "Just bring us a word."

FOR

the staff at Crawford Long Hospital, who welcomed the word.

FOR

Steve, Andy, Jenny, Hannah Ruth, and Soren,
who gave me encouragement, support, and space.

Resource Publications
A division of Wipf and Stock Publishers
199 W 8th Ave, Suite 3
Eugene, OR 97401

Spiritual Triage
Timely Meditations for Health-care Workers
By Nowicki, Karen A.
Copyright©2006 Pilgrim Press
ISBN 13: 978-1-60899-188-4
Publication date 11/16/2009
Previously published by Pilgrim Press, 2006

CONTENTS

1 ❦ Introduction

It's probably impossible to fully describe the amazing privilege of my work as a hospital chaplain. Every day on the job I'm blessed with stimulating company and fascinating events. Patients generously share their hospitality, hopes, and challenges with me, and staff members welcome me to their ministry of caregiving. I witness highly trained and vastly skilled professionals deal with bewildering situations, complicated procedures, hectic schedules, and unpredictable outcomes as ordinary parts of their workday. I see them encounter frightened patients, worried family members, anxious colleagues, bone-numbing fatigue, and daunting piles of paperwork. I've learned that health-care workers ride an emotional roller coaster, witnessing pain and sadness with one patient, alongside healing and joy with the next. I'm aware that they are apt to put their own exhaustion, hunger, and spiritual needs on hold while they meet the demands of the moment.

Spiritual Triage: Timely Meditations for Health-care Workers, is an attempt to respond pastorally to the pressures that can occur in the clinical workplace. Like medical triage, which addresses patients' needs in order of their severity, these interventions are intended to help keep health-care workers' spirits alive until there is time for more complete rest and reflection. They address several common elements of the health-care scene: the difficult challenges, the frequent lack of peace, the constant waiting, the surprising beauty, the occasional longing for silence, the desire for rest and renewal, the search for comfort and healing, the desire for hope, and the need for a caring community.

This collection of mediations is dedicated to all the nurses, technicians, custodial workers, doctors, nutritionists, unit clerks, administrative assistants, pharmacists, physical therapists, auxiliary volunteers, security officers, speech therapists, bookkeepers, respiratory therapists, lunchroom workers, administrators, and patients who teach me and each other how to survive and grow stronger in a well functioning and mutually supportive health-care community. May our spiritual stamina continue to increase as we work together toward greater healing.

Part One

MEETING CHALLENGES

Do not fear, for I am with you,
do not be afraid, for I am your God;
I will strengthen you, I will help you,
I will uphold you with my victorious right hand. ·

—Isaiah 41:10

Be strong and courageous;
do not be frightened or dismayed,
for the LORD your God is
with you wherever you go.

—Joshua 1:9

Conquering any difficulty always gives one
a secret joy, for it means pushing back a boundary-line
and adding to one's liberty.

—Henri-Frederic Amiel

1 ❧ Patients/Patience

*Be patient with everyone, but above all, with
yourself. I mean, do not be disheartened by
your imperfections, but always rise up with
fresh courage. How are we to be patient in
dealing with our neighbors' faults if we are
impatient in dealing with our own? She who
is fretted with her own failings will not
correct them. All profitable correction comes
from a calm, peaceful mind.*

— Saint Francis de Sales, 1567–1622

Marie sighed and rolled her eyes as she left the room. The
patient, although not nearly as ill as most others on the
unit, was difficult and demanding, and his family had been
downright rude. She might even say that they were impossible. They'd called her all day with angry questions, complicated requests, and bitter complaints. They never smiled
or said thank you. Marie had tried to practice patience
while balancing the wants of this patient with the needs of
the four other people she was looking after on her shift.
Her feelings of frustrations were escalating, and she feared
that that she was losing compassion for this patient. She

felt irritated by the situation and angry with herself for what seemed to be a loss of empathy.

An experienced nurse, she recognized anxiety when she saw it. She understood that this troubling patient and his family were especially frightened, and she wondered why, since his condition was far from life threatening. Upon being called to his room yet again, Marie fulfilled his many requests. She could hardly wait to leave the room, but somehow she paused long enough to ask if there were any further questions about the patient's condition or hospital procedures in general.

Their response revealed a source of their anxiety. Marie learned that up until now, this family had never experienced hospitalization. They saw hospitals not as places of healing, but as the last stop on the road of life. She addressed their worries and answered their questions as fully as time allowed, and then spent a few minutes attempting to get acquainted with them personally and letting them know a little about her own life. She admired a picture of their recent family reunion, and she told them a story about her baby granddaughter. When she left the room this time she felt better. She hoped that they did, too.

Gradually, the patient and his family began to trust the medical staff. Some of their fears slowly melted away, and they were able to accept the healing that was in process. The patient was discharged at the end of the week, but he didn't leave until he'd given Marie a hug.

❧ PRAYER FOR PATIENCE ❧

O God, it's true:
There are patients who try our patience.
They make unreasonable demands.
They scowl and growl;
they're surly, sour, strange.
They're angry and they're mean.
Bless them anyway, God,
and bless us as we learn to see your presence
in their questions, in their fears,
and in our power to care.
Amen

2 ❧ Satisfying Thirst

As a deer longs for flowing streams,
  so my soul longs for you, O God.
My soul thirsts for God, for the living God.
  When shall I come and behold the face of God?

—Psalm 42:1–2

It had been quite a week at the clinic. The patients had been especially numerous, ill, and needy. By Friday Caroline felt completely drained. She could hardly find the energy required to drive home, and she couldn't begin to imagine being able to return to work on Monday. But by the end of the weekend Caroline and her colleagues were ready to start all over again. Although they'd imagined that their sources of healing had dried up, they'd found that the streams were still flowing.

❧ DEEP NEED, BOTTOMLESS WELL ❧

Though distracted by the demands of the day,
immersed in intricate detail,
occupied by the needs of others,
still our souls recognize it:
a deep thirst for the Divine,
a longing for Sacred Company.
Guide us, Spirit.
Lead us to the spring,
walk us to the river,
quench our thirst.
Remind us that you're present,
that the well is never dry.
Amen

3 ❧ Freeing the Enemies

You prepare a table before me in the presence
of my enemies; you anoint my head with oil;
my cup overflows.

—PSALM 23:5

Sometimes there are enemies. They capture our attention and keep us from being all that we're meant to be. They follow us about and remind us of their presence. They interrupt our prayers, intrude their way into our meditations, and shadow us as we do our work. We find it challenging to be completely free of their power.

Our enemies come in various guises. Many times they dress up as feelings of anxiety, loss, self-doubt, lack of trust, fatigue, worry, and fear.

However our enemies appear, their presence often distracts us from the banquet table that God prepares for our nourishment and delight. That table is laden with beauty and blessings beyond imagining, but our fears can call us away from its joys.

We might not be able to completely banish enemies from our line of vision, but we can pray for the wisdom and courage to trust the beauty of the banquet more than we fear the presence of these unwanted guests.

❦ LIBERATION ❦

God of all,
in your company
we set free
the fears that prevent adventure,
the worries that block our vision,
the distress that hides joy.
In your presence
we learn peace.
Amen

4 ❧ Time to Fly

BE LIKE THE BIRD

Be like the bird, who
Halting in her flight
On limb too slight
Feels it give way beneath her,
Yet sings
Knowing she has wings.

—VICTOR HUGO

If I take the wings of the morning
and settle at the farthest limits of the sea,
even there your hand shall lead me . . .

—PSALM 139:9–10

"It was my first day to be charge nurse and I had a whole list of things that I was worried about. How would I care for my patients and manage the unit at the same time? Would I be able to make wise and fair decisions about assignments? What would I do if we had a code, or some other critical incident? What would happen if we were short staffed? Could I lead us through rounds efficiently and gracefully? Would everyone be able to take his or her break? Would I be able to finish giving report quickly enough to get home in time for my kids' return from school? I'd never had this much responsibility before and I was really nervous. I wanted to do it, but was I ready? I decided it was time for me to try my leadership wings, and sure enough, they were strong enough to carry me through."

❧ STRENGTH TO SOAR ❧

Gracious God of all,
in your holy presence
we find that we can soar.
Thank you for providing us with
strength beyond our expectation.
Amen

5 ❧ Mistakes

The LORD is gracious and merciful . . .
abounding in steadfast love.

— PSALM 145:8

But we make God's love too narrow
By false limits of our own,
And we magnify his strictness
With a zeal he would not own.

— F. W. FABER, "THERE'S A WIDENESS IN GOD'S MERCY"

To err is human, to forgive, divine.

— ALEXANDER POPE

In her white uniform and cap, Mrs. Harvey, the well-known and much-loved nursing supervisor of a large and respected teaching hospital, waited to approach the podium. Asked to speak about some of the most meaningful experiences of her forty-two years in health care, she was about to face an auditorium full of graduating nursing students. She'd prepared her speech carefully. She'd remembered the excitement of her own graduation and the challenges of the first several years of her career. She'd relived some of her more fascinating cases and most interesting patients. Although there were many lessons that Mrs. Harvey could share with her audience, she was amazed to realize that the most valuable ones had to do with those times where she'd fallen flat on her face and struggled to get up again. She'd been completely unprepared for her mistakes, yet they'd taught her so much. Like this year's class of new nurses, she'd been technically well-trained and prepared to carry out all kinds of clinical procedures in a professional, empathetic, ethical way, but she had been unequipped to deal with error. Her outline was ready.

DEALING WITH MISTAKES
Some Advice from a Voice of Experience

1. Know that mistakes happen in every workplace and recognize that they are especially challenging in a medical setting.

2. Always strive to avoid mistakes. Follow approved procedures; avoid hurry, distraction, and excessive fatigue.

3. Recognize error when it happens. Discuss it with all parties who need to know.

4. Assist staff in finding ways to remedy the situation.

5. Try to determine how the mistake happened. Think of ways to prevent it in the future.

6. If you are part of the mistake, apologize and ask for forgiveness.

7. This is the hardest part: forgive yourself. When you make a mistake, write it down, including all the painful details. Pray about it. Learn from it. When you're ready, tear it up and let it go.

8. Find dignity in the lessons you learn from mistakes.

❧ A PRAYER ❧

God of all situations,
be with us even in our mistakes.
Be with us as we recognize them.
Be with us as we talk about them.
Be with us as we examine them closely.
Be with us as we learn from them.
Be with us as we recover from them.
Be with us as we begin to hold them loosely.
Be with us as we learn to let them go.
Be with us as we grow into greater wisdom.
Be with us as we trust ourselves to trust in you.
Amen

Part Two

FINDING PEACE

Peace be within your walls,
and security within your towers.

—PSALM 122:7

Lord, make me an instrument of your peace.

—SAINT FRANCIS

For mercy has a human heart,
Pity a human face,
And love, the human form divine,
And peace, the human dress.

—WILLIAM BLAKE, "THE DIVINE IMAGE"

6 ❧ Hearing Peace

*Let me hear what God the LORD will speak, for
God will speak peace to the people.*

—PSALM 85:8

*Deep within us all there is an amazing inner
    sanctuary of the soul,
a holy place, a Divine Center, a speaking Voice,
to which we may continuously return.*

—THOMAS KELLY

It had been quite a day. There had been difficult patients,
tense situations, unexpected complications, numerous
lengthy telephone conversations, demanding paperwork,
no time for lunch, and a late start home. His head ached,
his feet hurt, he wondered how he'd ever gotten into this
line of work. He rushed to his car and joined the slow-
moving city traffic. He longed for the peace and quiet of
home but knew that it was going to be a slow commute. He
switched on the radio and then turned it off immediately,
realizing that he needed silence more than anything else.
His car crept past office buildings, apartments, and several

convenience stores. He saw a small leafy open space in the next block and decided to pull over and investigate. Parking his car on the side street, he walked into the little park. Finding a bench under an old oak, he sat down to revisit all the anxieties of the last ten hours.

After he'd recognized the tensions of the day and given them their due, he began to hold them less tightly. Not liking to be ignored, they gradually slunk away and he was finally free to access the sanctuary of his soul. For a while there, he'd forgotten about the peace of God's presence. He was glad that the traffic had slowed him down long enough to return him to awareness of divine company.

❧ A PRAYER ❧

God of all,
you are there
in the tension of our work,
in the anxieties of our schedules,
in the urgency of emergencies,
in the hurry of health care.
May we recognize your company in all that we do.
May we hear you speak of peace.
Amen

7 ❧ God's Face

My God, my God, why have you forsaken me?
Why are you so far from helping me, from the
words of my groaning?

—Psalm 22:1

Your face, LORD, do I seek.

—Psalm 27:8b

It was taking so long to get better. She'd been in the hospital for weeks. She missed her family, her friends, her home, her garden, her porch, her magnolia tree, her kitchen, her dog, and her church. She missed her life. She felt nothing but pain, grief, and emptiness. She'd prayed daily for God's presence, read scripture, and engaged in theological conversations, but still, God remained elusive. She felt separated from the Divine, abandoned by God.

Finally one morning God showed up, arriving with her nurse who'd come to check vitals and deliver medications. God was present in the way that her nurse cared for her. Suddenly she realized that God had been there all along, disguised as hospital staff. She began to notice further evidence of God's company: the shaft of sunlight that shone through the window onto the foot of her bed, the scent of the yellow rose on her bedside table, and the joy of the woman from nutritional services who sang *Amazing Grace* as she rolled the breakfast cart down the hall. God was there in the hospital community, and God was there, in her room and in her heart.

❧ A PRAYER ❧

Divine Comforter,
Lover of all souls,
Source of mercy,
Model of grace,
we seek your face.

We watch closely.
We catch glimpses of you
in familiar faces,
in the smile of a stranger,
and greatest gift of all:
We find you dwell in us.

In you we live fully
among the many faces
that bear your image.
Accept our thanks for all you are.
Amen

8 ❧ Peace in Stress

*We misunderstand the nature of peace if we think
of it as an ideal world, or as dependent on silence or
solitude; sooner or later, we have to admit reality —
with all its built-in anxieties.*

—Sister Wendy Beckett, *Book of Meditations*

Resurrection ferns are an amazing and ancient member of
the plant kingdom that grow on the branches of live oaks.
When they have the right amount of nutrients and mois-
ture they are green and fluttery like butterflies, but when
atmospheric conditions are harsh and punishing they become pale and stiff, looking as if they have no life left in
them. When the weather becomes more forgiving the dry,
seemingly lifeless fronds of the resurrection fern miracu-
lously return to their green and pliant selves again.

Members of the health-care community are a bit like
resurrection ferns. We like to move gracefully and work
smoothly, but the stresses and anxieties connected with a
medical setting occasionally render us weakened and
bland. Not liking to be in this state, we have various strate-
gies for coping and recuperation.

Sandy, who works in a very busy outpatient unit, has "island moments." When she senses that stress is about to stiffen her, she lets herself imagine that she's sitting on a sunny beach contemplating the movement of the waves. Upon her return from these brief retreats Sandy brings along some inner peace that helps her cope.

Crystal and her coworkers in another busy part of the hospital help each other cope by collecting ingredients for their "recipe for serenity." It's a work in progress. So far it calls for mutual encouragement, faith, deep breaths, prayer, and humor. They know that the recipe won't ban stress from their workplace, but they are clear that its contemplation brings them a certain sense of peace.

Like the resurrection fern, members of the hospital community have remarkable powers of renewal. We can't avoid the stress of a busy and hectic schedule, but we can find resilience and healing when we access our sources of inner peace.

ꙅ A PRAYER ꙅ

Can I do it?
Can I find a way?
Can I answer the call?
Can I fulfill the expectation?

Can I offer comfort
When I long for it myself?

Silence.
The tide is out.
There's nothing there but broken shells
and emptiness.

Let me sit a moment here with you.
Whisper something in my ear.
Remind me that I'm strong,
that the tide will rise again
and I will be refreshed.
Amen

9 ❧ A Peaceful Pace

God's delight is not in the strength of the horse,
nor God's pleasure in the speed of the runner;
but God takes pleasure in those who trust and
hope in God's steadfast love.

—PSALM 147:10–11

❧ A GRACEFUL GEAR ❧

We rush.
We worry.
We imagine urgency,
as if our worthiness
depends upon our speed.

There is another gear—
more graceful and more balanced,
which lets us breathe more deeply
and appreciate more fully
the pleasure of the Divine.

Holy One, may we have sufficient trust
to follow the rhythm of your delight.
Amen

A GUIDED MEDITATION

Stop.
Sit quietly, gently.
Let your body be light.
Listen. Feel. Breathe.
Welcome God's presence.

Let God see your strong parts.
Be thankful for strength.
Let God see your tender parts.
If there are wounds, let God touch them.

When you are ready, return to graceful, unhurried
    movement.
Be aware that in God's presence every moment is sacred
    and every space is holy.
Thanks be to God.

Part Three

WAITING

Let us, then, be up and doing,
With a heart for any fate;
Still achieving, still pursuing,
Learn to labor and to wait.

—HENRY WADSWORTH LONGFELLOW

But those who wait for the LORD
shall renew their strength,
they shall mount up with wings like eagles.

—ISAIAH 40:31

For God alone my soul waits in silence,
for my hope is from God.

—PSALM 62:5

10 ❧ Graceful Waiting

Wait for the LORD;
be strong, and let your heart take courage;
wait for the LORD!

—PSALM 27:14

The health-care community knows about waiting. We wait for arrivals, tests, results, procedures, decisions, medications, surgeries, therapies, rest, and comfort. And, like all other communities, we wait for healing. How can we do all this waiting with grace?

A health-care professional offers this advice:

"Use any downtime you can find to sit quietly with God and simply listen. Listen to the sounds outside, the beat of your heart, the tick of the clock, voices in the hall. Don't try to make anything special out of what you hear. Hold it all lightly and simply rest in the Divine Presence. End your meditation by feeling God's embrace. Let that carry you on to the rest of your day."

THE BEAUTY OF NOW

Sometimes we wait for the evening . . .
for home and familiar things.
Sometimes we wait for tomorrow
and the healing we hope it will bring.

We often imagine a future
much lovelier than the now.
We picture a time of great beauty,
we know it will come, but how?

May we in all of our waiting
slip gently close to you
and hear your whispered reminder:
"I'm present in all that you do."

In all for which we wait and pray,
in all we envision and dream,
your presence graces every second,
makes every moment gleam.

❧ A PRAYER ❧

God of all,
may your presence in our waiting
be healing, comforting, and strengthening.
Continue to bless our waiting with good company,
rewarding work, peace, creativity, and imagination.
Remind us to be grateful as we wait and pray.
Amen

11 ❧ Waiting for Wholeness

Because you have made the LORD your refuge,
the Most High your dwelling place,
no evil shall befall you, no scourge come near your tent.

—PSALM 91: 9–10

How do we, members of the health-care community who witness pain and illness as part of our everyday experience, live faithfully with the promises in this psalm? Sometimes our plans for healing aren't realized. Things seem to go wrong. Pain continues. Anxieties increase. Despite our most sincere attempts, a patient may not respond to our interventions. Healing, as we had imagined it, does not happen. How can we get beyond our own expectations of how God's promises might be fulfilled? How can we learn to see divine presence in clinical outcomes that don't match our hopes?

Psalm 27:14 advises us: "Wait for the LORD; be strong, and let your heart take courage, wait for the LORD." As we wait for the wisdom to see divine presence in all situations, we find the courage to see that God's idea of healing may transcend our own limited expectations. What appears to us as loss may be a kind of wholeness that is beyond our limited powers of recognition. May we learn to live trustingly in the mystery of God's wisdom.

❧   UNEXPECTED   ❧

God of lavish promises
and surprising fulfillment,
we welcome your presence
as we explore the unexpected paths
of your healing power.
Our hearts take courage
as we grow to trust
the mystery of your ways.
Amen

12   Letting God Be God

My help comes from the LORD
who made heaven and earth.

—PSALM 121:2

God expects one thing of you: that you should come
    out of yourself
insofar as you are a created being and let God
    be God in you.

—MEISTER ECKHART

Come down, O Love divine,
Seek thou this soul of mine,
And visit with thine own ardour glowing.
O Comforter, draw near,
Within my heart appear,
And kindle it, thy holy flame bestowing.

—BIANCO DA SIENA (DIED 1434)

Terri's job at the clinic is often stressful. Her duties call for precision and total focus, and at the end of the day she craves a change of pace. When she gets home she likes to get out her paints and let her artistic side have some exercise. Recently invited to show her work in a new gallery, she's been trying very hard to "be creative."

Last weekend she spent hours on countless preliminary sketches for a new painting, but none of them led to anything. She paced and worried and lost sleep. Then, remembering that creativity is a divine gift, she decided to spend some time in prayer and meditation. Having invited God's presence, she found that her painting was enriched. She said that the creative spirit was freed when she moved out of the way and let God be God in her.

❧ A PRAYER FOR CREATIVITY ❧

God of all creation,
in your company
every moment is holy,
and every space is sacred.
Remind us that we work
and rest most fully
when we recognize your presence
in everything we do.
Amen

Part Four

SEEING BEAUTY

*There is no excellent beauty that hath not
some strangeness in the proportion.*

— FRANCIS BACON

*All things counter, original, spare, strange;
Whatever is fickle, freckled (who knows how?)
With swift, slow; sweet, sour; adazzle, dim:
He fathers-forth, whose beauty is past change:
Praise him.*

— GERALD MANLY HOPKINS

13 ❧ Time for Dancing

Let us praise God's name with dancing,
making melody to God with tambourine and lyre.
For God takes pleasure in the people;
God adorns the humble with victory.

—PSALM 149:3–4

I cannot dance, O Lord,
Unless you lead me.
If you wish me to leap joyfully,
Let me see you dance and sing.

—MECHTILD OF MAGDEBURG, 1210–85

"As I child, I lived for my dance lessons. I waited all week for Saturday morning when I could go to class at the community center. I loved to leap and pirouette and glide around the gym while our teacher played the piano and counted out the steps for us. I felt strong and happy there, uplifted by the energy and the music. Sometimes, when things get tense at work, I remind myself that I'm still a dancer. I concentrate on keeping time to the rhythm of the hospital as I leap into patients' rooms. I let myself hear healing music as I pirouette and glide about taking vitals and giving medications. I think of my dance as a kind of moving meditation, a prayer for my patient and me as we grow together into greater wholeness."

DANCING WITH GOD *(a guided meditation)*

Hear sacred music.
Accept the invitation.
Embrace the Divine Partner.
Be held closely.
Feel God's pulse.
Move in time to the rhythm.
Leap, glide, sway.
Trust the healing of the dance.

Give thanks for greater wholeness.

14 ❧ Bright Beauty

Stir into flame the gift that is within you . . .

—SAINT PAUL

What lies behind us and what lies before us are tiny matters compared to what lies within us.

—RALPH WALDO EMERSON

You are the light of the world.

—JESUS

DIVINE LIGHTS *(a guided meditation)*

See the gleam
in the patient as she grows into healing.
See the light
in the nurse's bedside manner.
See the glow
as the doctor listens, reassures.
See the spark
of greeting in a smile.

See the brightness
in the community at work,
in the elevators, offices, labs, corridors,
operating suites, kitchen, waiting areas.
And the lamp within?
Can you see that, too?
Admire it.
Fan it.
Let it shine.
Give it air.
Let it breathe.
Nurture it as you work.
Let it guide your way.
Share it generously.

Your light warms us all.

15 ❧ Art at Work

*It is God's gift that all should . . . take pleasure
in all their toil.*

—Ecclesiastes 3:13

*Don't ask yourself what the world needs.
Ask what you need to do to come truly alive,
and then go and do that. What the world needs
is people who have come alive.*

—Howard Thurman

"How did I become a nurse? I couldn't help it. It's what I always wanted to do."

People with talent for caregiving often heed the call to medical work. They are highly trained and technically proficient, but more than that, they are artists whose work is divinely inspired. When they perform their art (the art of making a comfortable bed, giving injections, polishing floors, keeping records, preparing meals, doing surgery) they can feel truly alive because they're doing what they need to do to use the gifts that they've been given. Health-care workers find wholeness and vitality working in places where healing happens.

❧ ALIVE TO BEAUTY ❧

Divine Creator,
help us to remember that we
work best when we welcome you to
share our endeavors.

Remind us of the gift of our talents,
the beauty of our work,
the art of our labor,
the pleasure you take in our efforts.

May we come alive to your beauty
in our patients,
our colleagues,
and (most amazing of all) in ourselves.
Amen

16 ❧ Beholding Beauty

*One thing I asked of the LORD, that will I seek after:
to live in the house of the LORD all the days of my life,
to behold the beauty of the LORD, and to inquire in
    God's temple.*

—PSALM 27:4

It was their fifty-seventh wedding anniversary. His hospital room showed no outward signs of celebration. There were no cards, flowers, or balloons, yet the atmosphere seemed festive as they remembered the details of their wedding day.

He'd looked slender and handsome in a suit he'd borrowed from his brother.

Her dress was simple, white, and hand-sewn by her mother. She'd worn a small hat and carried carnations. He slowly opened his eyes, looked at her, and said,

"I can't recall the dress, but I do remember that you were beautiful."

They were quiet for a while as they enjoyed the flashback. Then she took his hand and answered,

"Everything can be beautiful when we remember our blessings—the old ones and the new."

ʂ   ABUNDANT BEAUTY   ʂ

God of mystery and mercy,
may we see your abundant beauty
as we live in the awareness of our blessings
and the reality of our need for healing.
May we walk bravely, trustingly, and gratefully
in the awesome beauty of your presence.
Amen

17 & The Symphony

Morning by morning God wakens—wakens
my ear to listen as those who are taught.

—Isaiah 50:4b

The medical workplace is filled with chaotic vibrations. Helicopters land on the roof. Sirens scream outside. Elevator doors swoosh open and shut. Carts rattle down the hall. Complicated equipment beeps insistently. Phones ring. Patients call out for their nurses. Visitors hurry noisily along corridors.

The din may be daunting to some, but health-care workers listen for God's voice in the roar that surrounds them. It can become music to their ears.

❧ HEARING GOD ❧

We hear you, God.

We hear you in the morning sounds:
Breakfast trays arriving,
doctors making rounds,
nurses giving report.

We hear you in the afternoon:
Visitors asking directions,
someone laughing,
someone anxious.

We hear you in the evening:
TV's turned to nightly news,
pillows being plumped,
psalms being read.

You speak your presence
in the symphony that surrounds us.
Thank you for each healing note.
Teach us to move gracefully
to the rhythm
of your composition.
Amen

Part Five

PRACTICING SILENCE

Elected silence, sing to me
And beat upon my whorled ear.
Pipe me to pastures still and be
The music that I care to hear.

—Gerald Manley Hopkins

Be silent, all people, before the LORD . . .

—Zechariah 2:13

18 ❧ In the Garden

They heard the sound of the LORD God walking
in the garden at the time of the evening breeze . . .

— GENESIS 3:8

How does she deal with tensions at work? A nurse reports:
"Last summer I was visiting friends in a big, noisy city.
I loved the excitement of the place, but after a while I began
to long for a quiet corner where I could catch my breath
and enjoy a little silence. I remember wandering down a
side street toward what appeared to be a leafy area behind
a huge church. The sign at the gate of the little park invited
me to enter and spend some time. I wandered along well-
worn stone paths, admired the plantings and the lily pond,
and found a bench surrounded by hollyhocks. The old oak
trees, the boxwood bushes, and the ivy-covered fence muf-
fled the sounds of the city. I'd found my breathing space. I
brought that park home with me and I visit it from time to
time when things get hectic at work. Even the shortest visit
revives me."

THE GARDEN *(a guided meditation)*

There's a garden where I go
to rest and calm my soul.
It isn't far away.
It's open every day.
Under an oak,
embraced by flower and vine,
I listen to the silence there,
and I remember peace.

You can go there too,
have a rest from all you do.
Slip gently from tension
to the silent space within.
Find a shady place to rest
or wander on the sunny paths.
Admire abundant beauty,
welcome God's embrace.
Rest, heal, revive.

19 ❧ Listening to Silence

Silence is a great help to a seeker after truth. In the attitude of silence the soul finds the path in a clearer light and what is elusive and deceptive resolves itself into crystal clearness. Our life is a quest after Truth, and the soul requires inward restfulness to attain its full height.

—MOHANDAS K. GANDHI

"I've always been a praying person. I schedule time for prayer each day. I'm accustomed to telling God about my gratitude, my needs, my worries, my errors, and my joys. I'm used to asking God to bless my family and friends. I also enjoy praying for strangers and all people everywhere in any kind of want or distress. However, since I've been here I've had time to experiment with another sort of prayer . . . a kind of prayer that doesn't involve words. In this sort of prayer I just sit quietly and let myself be open to the experience of God's company. I let my mind rest. Thoughts come to me, but I don't entertain them. I practice enjoying the presence of the Divine, dwelling in God's embrace. I think that praying in this way brings me into a fuller relationship with God.

"Earlier, I'd been doing all the talking. Now I'm being quiet and letting God get in a word or two" (quote from a hospice patient).

⸙ SACRED PRESENCE ⸙

Oh, Divine Creator,
whisper in our ears.
Remind us that you made us,
that you hold us very dear.

When we're not authentic,
when we lose the way,
Remind us of the sacredness
of each hour of every day.

May we have the courage
to rest silent in your heart
and listen to your symphony
so we can dance our part.
Amen

20 § Silent Sanctuaries

For God alone my soul waits in silence.

—Psalm 62:1

Rejoice with an indescribable and glorious joy . . .

—1 Peter 1:8b

Health care is seldom silent. Pagers beep, phones ring, announcements blare out of loudspeakers, patients chat in waiting rooms, air conditioners hum, and equipment squeaks and squeals. Health-care workers sometimes need an escape from all the noise and activity of the workplace. Knowing that God honors silence as well as sound, they look for ways to reach quiet places within themselves where words are unnecessary. They can access such sanctuaries in the rare moments they have between tasks.

﹩ UNUTTERABLE ﹩

How quickly put to words:
Our thoughts, our needs, our hopes,
our fears, our angst, our pain.
Just beneath the surface of ourselves
they find frequent verbal exercise.

Much harder to express:
The deep and silent awe,
the thundering quiet
of our challenges and hopes,
our greatest joys, our ecstasies.

Still, you hear them, God.
You listen closely
to our sighs, our longings,

and to our profound,
mute, unutterable
Hosannas.

We trust you to it all.
Amen

Part Six

REST AND RENEWAL

This above all: to thine own self be true,
And it must follow as the night the day,
Thou canst not be false to any man.

— SHAKESPEARE

And on the seventh day God finished
the work that God had done . . .

— GENESIS 2:2

Ah, why should life all labor be?

— ALFRED, LORD TENNYSON

21 § A Fresh Start

*Enter God's gates with thanksgiving, and God's courts
with praise. Give thanks to God, bless God's name.*

—PSALM 100:4

A photo of an elegant old garden gate hangs on a wall in
the staff locker room. Underneath it a handwritten sign
reads: "Swing open the gate to another day of hard work,
good company, and encounters with the unknown."

THE GATE OF THE DAY

The gate of the day swings open.
Stand at the threshold,
aware, awake, alive.
Let loose of old burdens.
Be free of the past,
unworried by the future.
Welcome the new beginning.
Embrace possibility.
Experience the view.
See spaces of challenge,
places of rest,
abundant light,
and cooling shadows.
Enter the courtyard grateful for
places to go
and places to stay.
God is present.
There is healing.
Trust the blessing of now.
Where are you called?
Begin in peace.
Move with grace.
Go with God.

22 ⚜ The Sacred Now

Look to the moment,
for it is life . . .
for yesterday is but a dream
and tomorrow is only a vision.
But the now, well lived
makes every yesterday a dream of happiness
and every tomorrow a vision of hope.

—ADAPTATION OF A SANSKRIT PROVERB

"I practice staying in the moment, but sometimes I stray. Our schedule is usually so full and busy that I can get distracted by all there is to do. For instance, when I'm with a patient and there are several others waiting, I find it hard to be fully present to that one because I'm already anxious about the needs of the next person. So I keep reminding myself that every moment is sacred and worthy of my full attention. I do my best work and I'm happiest when I'm faithful to the task of the moment."

A GUIDED MEDITATION

Are there distractions?
Acknowledge them.
Examine them fully.
Hold them loosely.
When you're ready, let them go.
Be free.
Be silent.
Breathe into the present.
When intrusions come,
set them free.
Be faithful to the moment.
Know its sacredness.
Experience its wonder.
Feel gratitude.
See that in God's company,
all time is holy.
Be present in the now.

23   **A b o u t   O u r   W o r k**

Blessed be the LORD who daily bears us up . . .

—PSALM 68:19

What we say about our work: quotes from health-care workers:

"It's rewarding."

"It's exhausting."

"I like to make a difference."

"When I first started I was so scared, but I kept coming back because I always wanted to do this work, and nothing was going to stop me."

"Some situations seem impossible."

"There are patients that are difficult."

"There are patients that are inspiring."

"There are patients that I'll always remember."

"Sometimes the best part of the day is going home."

"My colleagues support me and trust me."

"Some days everything is on the edge of limbo."

"What matters most is knowing that I've done my best."

"The tension can be rough, but I love the healing that happens."

"I've tried to do other kinds of work, but it just isn't me."

ꙹ   A PRAYER FOR THE WORKPLACE   ꙹ

God of all,
each day at work you honor us with your company.
When we abide in your presence
our work becomes dance,
our routines, liturgies of praise,
our conversation, music,
our record keeping, written prayer.

Your presence
comforts us in painful times,
strengthens us in frustrating moments,
encourages us when we're low,
guides us through challenging situations,
refreshes us with laughter, and
embraces us when we need rest.

Blessed be the LORD, who daily bears us up.
Amen

24 ❖ Stairwell Sanctuary

So I have looked upon you in the sanctuary, beholding your power and glory.

—Psalms 63:2

Where is sanctuary? One staff member finds it in the quiet of a back stairwell. If you're there at the right time, there's a chance you might hear her singing.

Her calling is to be a caregiver. She finds meaning in her work with patients and colleagues, and she also finds fatigue, so she renews her energy by spending part of her break time sitting on the steps listening to God, praying and singing. Sometimes she sings the blues, and sometimes she sings for joy. Whatever the reason for her song, she trusts God to welcome it and to listen to its message.

After a visit to her sanctuary she returns to work refreshed and reminded that she has sufficient stamina (both physical and spiritual) to do her work with verve and grace. She feels that self-care is part of her job as a nurse, and on the days when her schedule is too hectic to visit her sanctuary she finds refuge in knowing that God can find her wherever she is.

◈ SACRED SPACE ◈

Divine Comforter, Lover of all souls, in you we find sanctuary.
When we're anxious
Your presence is calming.
When we're exhausted,
you are our rest.
When we're empty,
you fill our souls.
When we're confused,
you listen and guide.
When we're discouraged,
your embrace is strengthening.
When we hurt,
you give us space to heal.

Divine Comforter, Lover of all, we find refuge and
    refreshment in you.
Amen

Part Seven

ASKING QUESTIONS

What is the answer? . . .
In that case, what is the question?

—GERTRUDE STEIN

Hear, and I will speak; I will question you,
and you declare to me.

—JOB 42:4

Weary the path that does not challenge.
Doubt is an incentive to truth
and patient inquiry leadeth the way.

—HOSEA BALLOU (1796–1861)

*Ask and it will be given to you; search, and you
will find. . . . For everyone who asks receives, and
everyone who searches finds . . .*

—MATTHEW 7:7–8

Dr. S., a silver-haired retired English professor, spent hours
everyday pacing about the neuro-psych unit of the geriatric
hospital. Diagnosed with dementia, he hadn't spoken or in-
teracted with anyone in several months. Other patients,
staff, and his family had grown used to his silent agitation.
None of their attempts to communicate had succeeded and
they could think of nothing else to do but leave him to his
solitary rounds.

One morning a staff member, thinking there was nothing to lose, decided to accompany Dr. S. as he wove his way
through the large common area. Knowing that he was
steeped in literature, she recited pieces of some poetry that
she'd memorized over the years. This made no impression
on Dr. S., but he didn't seem to mind her company. The
nurse, striding briskly to match Dr. S.'s pace then asked,

"So, who's your favorite poet?"

Dr. S. stopped in his tracks. He made eye contact with
his questioner. He looked away, and then focused again.

"T. S. Eliot," he said, pausing a moment before striding on.

Immediately, the entire unit tuned into what had just happened. The unit clerk looked up from her word processor. A doctor paused attentively. Some of the patients appeared to notice that something unusual had happened. Someone had asked the right question and Dr. S. had spoken. His caregivers now knew that important parts of his true self were still available. They began to read to him from some of his old books and were delighted to see Dr. S. sit peacefully, and nod and smile as he listened to familiar verses. The right question had brought a measure of peace and healing.

ৡ HOLY CURIOSITY ৡ

God of comfort and source of all health,
you bring us patients with paths to travel
and stories to tell.
Abide with us
as we accompany them
patiently, curiously, respectfully
on their journeys.
Stay with us
as we learn
to ask questions that expose truth
and reveal strength.
Be near us
as we listen carefully to the answers.
Dwell with us
while we grow into healing.
Amen

26 ❧ Who May Abide?

O LORD, who may abide in your tent?
Who may dwell on your holy hill?

—PSALM 15:1

Occasionally, when the air seems clear and we aren't too distracted by everyday concerns, we can almost make out that big and beautiful tent on top of the not too distant hill. We intend to travel closer to it. Often the road seems to be taking us in that direction. Sometimes we're almost near enough to hear inviting sounds coming from under the canvas cover: an orchestra warming up; a choir practicing; tables being set; people laughing and talking like they do when they're with friends.

It would be great to abide in such a place. However, we question our worthiness and we wander away from the view. Sometimes we completely forget about the tent because we're so focused on our duties, doubts, and failings.

Who may abide in the tent on the holy hill? May we be curious enough to creep close, bold enough to open the flap, brave enough to step inside, and wise enough to know that there is room inside for all who seek a place.

A GUIDED MEDITATION

Find a quiet corner.

Breathe gently.

Be present in the now.

Let go of the past and the future.

Be in this moment.

Visualize the tent.

In it is that which you want most deeply.

Free yourself from all that would prevent you from dwelling there.

Is there anxiety? Offer it to God.

Is there lack of trust? Offer it to God.

Is there fatigue, anger, guilt? Let that go, too.

Find your place in the tent.

Rest there.

Notice all you can notice.

Accept it gently.

Be unhurried.

Be grateful.

Return to work refreshed.

27 § Welcome, Mystery

I want to beg you as much as I can . . . to be patient toward all that is unsolved in your heart and to try to love the questions themselves. . . . Do not seek answers which cannot be given to you because you would not be able to live them. And the point is to live everything. Live the questions now. Perhaps you will then, gradually, without noticing it, live along some distant day into the answer.

—Ranier Maria Rilke

God moves in a mysterious way, His wonders to perform . . .

—William Cowper, 1731–1800

He couldn't believe it was happening. He'd faced it all before with courage, prayer, and chemotherapy. It had been the hardest thing he'd ever done. He'd won that battle and now it looked as if he had to fight it all over again. He wondered why. His family wondered why. His health-care team wondered why. They had many questions as they planned their strategy for medical intervention.

❧ A PRAYER ❧

God of mystery,
our work involves so many questions:
Why is this happening?
What is the diagnosis?
How will treatment proceed?
When will healing begin?
Where do we look for answers?

Help us to see your presence
in the spaces where we do the asking.
Help us to welcome your company
as we wait for answers.
Help us to live faithfully with the questions
as we grow together into greater wholeness.
Amen

28 ❦ Unsearchable God

For my thoughts are not your thoughts,
nor are your ways my ways, says the LORD.

—Isaiah 55:8

God's greatness is unsearchable.

—Psalm 145:3

A health-care worker wonders, "Working with all of these sick people, sometimes I feel overawed by my own health. I mean, who am I to be so blessed?"

❧ UNACCOUNTABLE BLESSINGS ❧

We try to account for the fact
that our blessings far exceed
our goodness.
We want to add things up,
balance the books,
find the bottom line,
deserve the largesse.

We ponder, strive,
grapple, theorize.

And then we begin to abide,
curiously,
gratefully
generously,
trustingly,
gracefully,
peacefully
in the Vast, Divine Unknown.

Divine Comforter, Lover of all souls, may we grow
unsuspicious of our blessings. May we use them in
ways that spread joy, celebrate community, and
enhance healing.
Amen

Part Eight

COMFORT AND HEALING

God will wipe away every tear from their eyes.
Death will be no more;
mourning and crying and pain
will be no more, for the first things
have passed away.

—REVELATION 21:4

Heal me, O LORD, and I shall be healed . . .

—JEREMIAH 17:14

29 ❦ Welcome, God

Where can I go from your spirit? Or where can I flee from your presence? . . . If I take the wings of the morning and settle at the farthest limits of the sea, even there your hand shall lead me and your right hand shall hold me fast.

—PSALM 139:7, 9–10

❧ A PRAYER ❧

Thank you, Creator of all, for your presence
in the sometimes painful privilege
of working in a place where healing happens.
Your company helps us move through challenging, anxious,
        and stressful times with grace, humor, and dignity.
In your presence our tasks become dances of grace,
our routines, rituals of healing,
and our paperwork, written prayer.
You are with us on the days when we're bold and strong
and on the days when we feel weak and vulnerable.
We gain courage from knowing that you facilitate our
        daily schedules
and bless our work and our rest.
Thank you for opportunities to offer hospitality
to those who come to us for relief and healing.
May we continue to welcome patients and their families
        to our workplace
and may we always welcome your presence here too,
God of hospitality, comfort, and healing.
Amen

30 ❧ **A Healing Spirit**

Where can I go from your spirit?
Or where can I flee from your presence?

—Psalm 139:7

Come Holy Spirit, God and Lord;
Be all thy gifts in plenty poured
To save, to strengthen, and make whole
Each ready mind, each waiting soul.

—Martin Luther, 1524

My hands work for healing, yes, and they work best
when I invite the spirit to guide them.

—A HOSPITAL STAFF MEMBER

❧ **INVITING SPIRIT** ❧

Come and visit us, Holy Spirit:
Come and pray in us,
come and dance in us,
come and cry in us,
come and sing in us,
come and laugh in us.

Come and heal our emptiness:
Fill us with gratitude,
supply us with imagination,
bless us with patience,
satisfy us with peace,
replenish us with trust.

Come and dwell in us, Holy Spirit:
Teach us delight,
instruct us in grace,
school us in love.
Help us know your presence.
Amen

31 ❧ Visions of Comfort

Let your steadfast love become my comfort . . .

—Psalm 119:76

Comfort, *from a Greek word meaning*
called alongside.

He'd been very sick. He could remember nothing about those first two weeks in the intensive care unit except the vivid dreams. In them, he'd seen angels dressed in green gowns surrounding his bed. They flapped their wings, they sang, they prayed, and they provided a strange and gentle comfort. The dreams stopped when he began to come back to himself and notice that his doctors and nurses looked very familiar, as if he'd met them before. Gradually, he recognized them as the guardian angels of his dreams. They still wore those green gowns, but where had they hidden their wings?

❦ CALLED TO COMFORT ❦

Holy Comforter,
Lover of all,
you call us alongside of our patients.
Your spirit moves in us,
teaching compassion,
engendering trust,
offering peace.
As we provide comfort for others
we are aware of our own need for healing.
We find the solace of your Divine Assistance
in all that we do.
Amen

32 ❧ Unexpected Healing

O Lord, heal me, for my bones are shaking with terror.

—Psalm 6:2b

Alice was a petite, lively thirty-two-year-old with an easy smile, a whimsical sense of humor, and an earnest desire to be healthy. Her room was decorated with the colorful artwork of her kindergarten students and a banner that read "Get well soon, Mrs. Greene, we miss you." Alice was paying attention to that sign, and she believed that she was getting better every day. Her doctors believed it too and were planning to discharge her at the end of the week. Suddenly things changed. In spite of what had seemed to be great promise, Alice's symptoms reoccurred, and it became clear that she wouldn't recover. Staff could only make her comfortable and try to find ways to cope with their sad frustration.

Alice's story illustrates one of the challenging truths of health care: the fact that despite much promise, a positive prognosis, and our most sincere attempts, patients sometimes fail to respond to our interventions. How can we find divine presence in clinical outcomes that don't match our expectations and hopes?

Psalm 27:14 advises: "Wait for the LORD; be strong, and let your heart take courage, wait for the LORD!" Maybe, as we wait for the wisdom to see divine presence in all situations, we can find courage enough to imagine that God's idea of healing may transcend our own limited expectations. Maybe, in God's company, loss can become wholeness.

❦ GROWING INTO HEALING ❦

Source of wholeness,
we welcome your presence
as we travel the unexpected paths
of your healing.
Our hearts take courage
as we grow to trust
the beauty of your company
and the mystery of your ways.
Amen

33 ❧ A Patient's Song

I will sing to the LORD . . .

—Exodus 15:1B

How could we sing the LORD's song in a foreign land?

—Psalm 137:4

"It was hard, at first. It took a while to get used to the whole culture of the place. I felt as if I were in a foreign country . . . all that odd looking equipment, the unusual sounds and smells, the untranslatable medical language. I wondered how I'd be comfortable in such unfamiliar surroundings. I was awkward and uneasy until I began to make friends with the place and the staff. The hospitality of my doctors, nurses, and technicians helped me relax into healing. When I started my treatments I was singing the blues, but in the end I sang a different song" (quote from a chemotherapy patient).

❧ A PRAYER FOR OUR PATIENTS ❧

Source of all healing,
when our patients feel as if they're stranded
in hostile and unfamiliar territory,
may our company
be comforting to them.
When they feel awkward,
may we help them find grace.
When they forget how to sing their songs,
may we help them find the melody.
When they're unaware that you are with them,
May they find your presence in our care.
Amen

Part Nine

DEEPENING HOPE

But I will hope continually,
and will praise you yet more and more.

—Psalm 71:14

Do you have hope for the future?
Someone asked Robert Frost, toward the end.
Yes, and even for the past, he replied,
That it will turn out to be all right
For what it was.

—David Ray, "Thanks, Robert Frost"

34 ✦ The Thing with Feathers

Let your steadfast love, O LORD, be upon us,
even as we hope in you.

—PSALM 33:22

Hope is the thing with feathers
That perches on the soul,
And sings the tune without the words,
And never stops at all

—EMILY DICKINSON "HOPE IS THE THING WITH FEATHERS"

Even with all of its challenging realities, the health-care setting can be a place where hope runs rampant. Hope can comfort, inspire, and promote healing. It can bring energy to impossible situations and peace to the pain of transition and loss. Hope can exert its force in surprising and unexpected ways. Hope can be obvious and unavoidable, and it can be elusive and mysterious. Sometimes we have to find a quiet moment and wait for hope to perch on our soul. Often it lands so lightly that we don't even know it's there until we begin to hear the whisper of its tune.

❧ THANKS FOR HOPE ❧

Divine Comforter:
We hear discord.
We witness transition.
We see pain.
We encounter loss.

You provide courage.
You inspire hope.
You help us carry the load.
You hear our fears.
You offer words of healing.
You fill our emptiness with your presence.
You are with us on the path to peace.
Accept our hopes and prayers,
our thanks and praise.
Amen

35 ❧ Resurrections

I will give them one heart,
and put a new spirit within them;
I will remove the heart of stone
from their flesh and give them a heart of flesh.

—EZEKIEL 11:19

He'll always remember that Easter Sunday two years ago when his pager went off before sunrise telling him to come to the hospital immediately. A heart had become available, and if all went well he'd receive the transplant he'd been awaiting for so many months.

He approached the hospital with fear and joy. He saw himself starting a new life and he wondered what it would be like. Well aware that it was Easter, he envisioned a kind of personal resurrection.

The surgery was successful. The pain is past and he's made a new beginning. As he grows into healing, he finds that he has received blessings well beyond his ability to imagine.

Like this patient, we all have the potential to discover our own resurrections and healings. We can watch for God to act in surprising ways that exceed the powers of

our vision. Every day becomes like Easter when we experience evidence of God's lavish love in unexpected places
and unusual circumstances.

❧ HOLY SPACES ❧

Divine Creator, Comforter, Healer,
we meet you in all the holy spaces:
You're there at the points of mystery,
you listen to our doubts,
you're available when we hurt.

We ask for faith enough to watch for you
in all times and circumstances,
trusting you in the mystery,
finding you in the doubt,
accepting your healing.

Your presence makes
sacred time of all the moments of our lives,
and blesses all we do.
Amen

36 ❧ A Future with Hope

For surely I know the plans I have for you,
* says the LORD,*
plans for your welfare and not for harm,
to give you a future with hope.
Then when you call upon me and come and pray to me,
I will hear you.

—JEREMIAH 29:11–12

"I don't know what tomorrow will be like,
but I know God will be there"
(said by a patient on the eve of his surgery).

❦ SOURCE OF HOPE ❦

God of all,
we hear sighing,
we witness pain,
we feel tension,
we encounter loss.

You provide courage.
You inspire hope.
You hear our fears.
You help us carry the load.
You offer words of healing.
You fill us with your presence.
You join us on the path to wholeness.

Accept our hopes and prayers,
our vision and our dreams,
our thanks and praise.
Amen

37 ❦ Work and Hope

Commit your work to the LORD . . .
The human mind plans the way,
but the LORD directs the steps.

— PROVERBS 16:3, 9

"I wanted to be a nurse ever since I was a kid. I love my work. I'm good at it. I like to be with people, visit with them and their families, watch them heal. Still, there are times I'd rather stay home. That's when I pray myself through the day. Well, I guess I always pray myself through the day, but sometimes I pray a little harder than usual" (quote from Ralph, R.N.).

❧ A PRAYER ❧

Good morning, God.
Thank you for bringing on another day.

Time to get ready for work—
Work that's fun, rewarding, challenging—
Work I've always wanted to do.

But today, God, help me,

I'd rather stay home.
I'd rather sleep late,
take a walk in the rain,
clean the hall closet,
read a book,
make some soup,
water the plants,
call a friend,
play the piano,
write a letter,
groom the dog,
wash the car,
take a nap,
watch the light come through the windows,
rest, relax, reflect.

OK, God.
I'm putting my feet on the floor
and I'm hoping you can help me take it from there.
Here we go.
Amen

Part Ten

CELEBRATING COMMUNITY

Don't walk behind me; I may not lead.
Don't walk in front of me; I may not follow.
Just walk beside me and be my friend.

—ALBERT CAMUS

O magnify the LORD with me,
and let us exalt God's name together.

—PSALM 34:3

38 § The Work of Our Hands

Let the favor of the LORD our God be upon us, and
prosper for us the work of our hands — O prosper
the work of our hands!

—PSALM 90:17

A HAND BLESSING

May our hands and all that they do be blessed.
May they be strong, creative, and gentle.
May the Spirit guide them.
May they provide comfort and healing.
May their touch remind patients of God's divine grace
    and mercy.
May they work with compassion, and may they also play
    and rest in good measure.
May they feel beauty, create peace, and clap with joy.
May our hands and all that they do be blessed.

❧ A PRAYER ❧

Thank you, Creator of all, for the challenge and privilege of working in a place where healing happens.

Thank you for your presence in our work and for the knowledge that you are with us on the days when we feel bold and strong and on the days when we feel weak and vulnerable.

Thank you for the courage that comes from knowing that you facilitate our daily routines and that you bless our work and our rest.

Thank you for opportunities to offer hospitality to those who come here for relief and healing.

May we continue to welcome patients and their families to our place of work and may we always welcome your presence here too, God of hospitality, hope, comfort, and healing.

Amen

39 § **A l o n e**

I am like a lonely bird on the housetop.

—Psalm 102:7b

But how can one keep warm alone?

—Ecclesiastes 4:11b

THE NIGHT SHIFT

Doing paperwork alone, in that cold, artificial light,
hearing the moans of painful sleep,
witnessing midnight on Main Street from a curtainless
    window,
walking a deserted corridor at 2 A.M.,
no visitors, no footsteps, no laughter,
I understand what loneliness is.

Although there are many people at work at the hospital all
times of the night and day, it is still possible for health-care
workers to feel alone. Often feelings of solitude are welcome and peaceful, but at other times being alone can
seem cold and empty. A fine thing about the health-care
scene is that being on our own is only a temporary condi-

tion. When we think we might not make it through another lonely night shift, when we realize we need some human companionship, when the load is too heavy to carry alone—that's when we remember that we're all in this together. We hear voices around the corner, we smell bacon cooking for early breakfast, or we glimpse familiar figures emerging from an elevator and we know that we can make it because we're not alone. The energy that comes from being together helps us get the work done.

♠ WORKING TOGETHER ♠

God of all, thank you for the opportunity of working in a
    place of healing
where your presence is evident in our patients, our
    colleagues,
and even in ourselves.
In your Holy Company we learn to work together,
gracefully, through our daily routines.
Amen

40 ⚜ **Teamwork**

Beloved, you do faithfully whatever you do
for the friends . . .

—3 John 5

Friendship is Love without his wings.

—Lord Byron

A patient told the following story to illustrate his experience at the hospital.

"We were visiting my sister, who lives in a rural area overlooking a river. As we sat on her porch having lunch we could hear the honking of geese as they flew north for the summer. A small "v" formation of three geese landed in the river. After they'd had some rest they noisily flapped their wings and rose to continue their trip. They circled three times, each time rising higher over the porch and river. On the third circle one of the geese caught a foot on the power line and tumbled to the ground. The other two continued their flight. Wondering how we could help, we put the very curious hunting dogs in the house and waited to see what would happen.

"In a few minutes the two geese returned to check on their companion. They called out to her and she flapped her wings, rising to join them. Again she encountered the power line and fell to earth, and again the two others continued their flight, returning several minutes later. They circled many times honking encouragement to their grounded flight-mate. At last she found the strength to test her wings and rose in three uncertain spirals, finally clearing the power line. The "v" of three, honking loudly, continued their journey. We could see the rescued goose gaining confidence and altitude as her wings began to regain the rhythm of flight. Being in the hospital is something like being that third goose. I'm down, but my family and the hospital staff are staying with me while I gain the strength to continue my life's journey. When it's time, I'll fly again."

❧ GOOD COMPANY ❧

Your holy company
enables us to offer companionship
to our colleagues and
to all who come to us for healing.
Glory to you,
Spirit and friend.
Together, we find strength in the shadow of your wings.
Amen

41 ♣ Trust

Trust the LORD with all your heart,
and do not rely on your own insight.
In all your ways acknowledge God,
and God will make straight your paths.

—PROVERBS 3:5–6

Recently a patient revisited the above scripture and found that it spoke to her more clearly than it had before. She said:

"I've always been a hard worker. I set goals, get up early, and accomplish things. I like to think that I can rely on myself . . . well, I can, but since I've been in the hospital I've discovered that I can do even better. I've learned that I can rely on others, too. I can rely on the training and expertise of those who care for me. I can rely on the wisdom and support of my family and my friends. And I can rely on God's healing power. I'm not alone in my medical and spiritual situation. I'm a team member in our work for the greater good."

❧ FOR TRUST ❧

Divine Spirit,
Holy Comforter,
Lover of all souls,
You accompany us
In every challenge, every celebration.

We trust
our training,
our skill,
our strengths,
our instincts,
each other.
We trust you
and we embrace your companionship
in every step toward healing.
Amen

42 ❧ Gratitude

Sing praises to the LORD,
O you his faithful ones,
and give thanks to God's holy name.

—PSALM 30:4

A LITURGY OF THANKS

For family, friends, neighbors, and colleagues,
we give you thanks, O God.

For work to do in a place of healing,
we give you thanks, O God.

For food that nourishes our bodies,
For words that nurture our souls,
For ideas that stimulate our minds,
we give you thanks, O God.

For fresh air, clear water, and comfortable shelter,
we give you thanks, O God.

For health, strength, and spirit,
We give you thanks, O God.

For the courage to live with our convictions,
For the faith to find your presence in challenging situations,
For the wisdom to care for ourselves as well as we care for
    others,
We give you thanks, O God.

For these blessings and all others,
We give you thanks and praise.

Amen